# CROWS

by Natalie Lunis

Consultant: Karl Kranz
General Curator
The Maryland Zoo in Baltimore

PUBLISHING COMPANY, INC.

New York, New York

## Credits

Cover (center), NHPA/T. Kitchin & V. Hurst; Cover (background), Davorin Pavlica/
istockphoto; Title page, NHPA/T. Kitchin & V. Hurst; 4–5, Courtesy of The Behavioural
Ecology Research Group, Department of Zoology, Oxford University; 6–7, Courtesy of
Gavin Hunt, The Department of Psychology, University of Auckland, New Zealand, http://
www.psych.auckland.ac.nz; 8, Dave Herring; 9, © Michael Quinton/Minden Pictures;
10, NHPA/Bill Coster; 11, David J. Slater/Alamy Pictures; 12, © Usher & Lamm/Foto
Natura/Minden Pictures; 13 (top), Robert H. Armstrong/Animals Animals, Earth Scenes;
13 (bottom), MC Donald Wildlife Photos/ Animals Animals, Earth Scenes; 14, Gary
Zahm/Bruce Coleman USA; 15, D. Hurst/ Alamy; 16, © DANISH ISMAIL/Reuters/
Corbis; 17, Paul Hobson/Naturepl.com; 18, John T. Fowler/Alamy; 19, Art Wolfe/Photo
Researchers, Inc.; 20, Jean-Claude Carton/Bruce Coleman USA; 21, Stockbyte Silver/
Alamy; 22, Edgar T. Jones/Bruce Coleman USA; 23, NHPA/Manfred Danegger; 24, Mike
Lane/Alamy; 25, NHPA/Manfred Danegger; 26, © Ron Niebrugge/wildnatureimages.
com; 27, David Tipling/Alamy; 28 (left), Joe McDonald/Bruce Coleman USA; 28 (right),
Stephen J. Krasemann/Photo Researchers, Inc.; 29, The Granger Collection.

Design and production by Dawn Beard Creative and Octavo Design and Production, Inc.

*Library of Congress Cataloging-in-Publication Data*

Lunis, Natalie.
  Crows / by Natalie Lunis.
    p. cm.—(Smart animals!)
  Includes bibliographical references and index.
  ISBN-13: 978-1-59716-160-2 (library binding)
  ISBN-10: 1-59716-160-8 (library binding)
  1. Crows—Juvenile literature. 2. Animal intelligence—Juvenile literature. I. Title.
II. Series.

  QL696.P2367L86 2006
  598.8'64—dc22

                        2005026830

For more information, write to Bearport Publishing Company, Inc., 101 Fifth Avenue,
Suite 6R, New York, New York 10003. Printed in the United States of America.

10 9 8 7 6 5 4 3 2

# Contents

# Brainy Betty

Betty had a problem. A tempting piece of meat was lying in a little bucket at the bottom of a plastic tube. She could not reach the meat with her **beak**, however. The tube was too long. What could she do to get it?

▲ **This is Betty, a New Caledonian crow. New Caledonia is an island in the Pacific Ocean.**

Fortunately, there was a piece of wire nearby. Betty tried to use it to get the meat. At first she failed. Then she bent the wire into a hook. She lowered the hook into the tube and pulled out the little bucket.

Betty was no birdbrain. She had solved her problem by making a **tool**.

Crows have strong, pointy beaks. Betty used her beak to make the hook.

◀ **Betty pulls up the bucket. Inside is a piece of pig heart, her favorite food.**

# A Brand-New Tool

Betty lived at a science lab at Oxford University in England. The scientists who took care of her knew a lot about crows and how smart they are. They knew that crows like Betty make and use tools in their natural **habitat**.

ASNNC

*outil*

Nou
Caléd

70 F

J-R LISIAK

"Corbeau calédonien" *Corvus moneduloides et ses O*

ITVF

▲ Making tools is a sign of a smart animal. This stamp honors crows and their skills at making and using tools to get food.

The scientists had set up the plastic tube, the little bucket, and the wire as an **experiment**. They wanted to see if a crow was smart enough to make a tool out of a strange new material. Betty hadn't let them down. She'd passed the test with flying colors.

◀ New Caledonian crows make little spears out of leaves. They use the spears to poke and pull out insects that are hidden in trees.

Chimpanzees make and use tools to get food, too. However, they were unable to make a tool like Betty's when they took the same test.

▲ Crows also use twigs to get bugs out of trees.

# One Smart Family

If there were a smart animal hall of fame, crows would definitely be in it. So would several of their close relatives, including ravens, jays, and magpies. All these birds, along with crows, belong to the **corvid** family.

## Where American Crows Live

Range of the American crow

▲ Members of the corvid family live all over the world. The most common crow in North America is called the American crow. This map shows where it lives.

Like crows, ravens have done well on tests designed by scientists. In one test, a raven looked at a group of six objects. The bird picked the object that did not belong because it was shaped differently from the rest.

There are over 100 **species**, or kinds, of birds in the corvid family. Ravens are the largest corvids in North America.

▲ Ravens look a lot like crows. They also are very clever. This raven is opening a pouch on a motorcycle to find out what's inside.

# In the Wild

Crows don't show their **intelligence** only on tests. They also show how smart they are in their everyday lives.

Sometimes crows trick smaller birds. The crows imitate the sounds of hawks, owls, and other dangerous **predators**. When the smaller birds become frightened and take off, the crows snatch their food.

Crows are excellent **mimics**. They can imitate the sound of a dog, a cat, a human voice, or even a cell phone.

▲ **Crows can use their voices to play tricks on others.**

At other times, crows warn one another of danger. When a group of crows looks for food on the ground, one or two often perch on a tree. They seem to act as lookouts. If they spot danger and let out a warning call, the other crows fly to safety.

◀ Hawks and other birds hunt crows for food.

# Finding Food

Crows are not picky eaters. They will eat almost anything, including seeds, nuts, fruit, insects, meat, fish, and eggs. Crows hunt frogs, mice, and other small creatures. They are also **scavengers** who feed on **roadkill** and other dead animals.

▲ Crows and other scavengers are nature's clean-up crews. They help clear away dead animals by eating them.

Crows have clever ways of getting the many foods they eat. They will drop a nut with a hard shell from high in the air to crack it open. They sometimes pull up people's fishing lines and eat the fish that have been hooked.

◀ **This crow drops a shell to crack it open and get the food inside.**

*upper mandible*

*lower mandible*

Sometimes two crows team up as partners to get food. One partner gets the attention of another bird or animal that is eating. The other crow then swoops in to steal the food.

▲ **A crow's beak has two main parts, which are called *mandibles*. Crows can use their beaks to pick up, hold, crack, or tear their food.**

# Outsmarting Scarecrows

One food crows love to eat is corn. So farmers started making **scarecrows** to keep crows out of cornfields. A scarecrow is meant to look like a person guarding the field.

Crows are too smart to be tricked by these big stuffed dolls, however. They quickly figure out that the scarecrow is harmless and go on eating the corn.

Recently, a farmer in Arizona had a new idea for scaring off crows. He put a radio in his cornfield and blasted rock-and-roll music at them. Unfortunately, his idea did not work. Crows kept coming to eat the corn. They even started moving to the rock-and-roll beat!

◄ **Farmers know that scarecrows don't really scare crows. Today most scarecrows are put up as decorations.**

Some companies have started making high-tech scarecrows. The scarecrows light up, give off sirens, and wave their arms and legs.

◄ **Crows feeding in a cornfield**

# Staying in Touch

Scientists have found that smart animals tend to be very **social**. They live in groups where they work together and help one another.

Crows are social birds. They help each other find food and stay safe. Sometimes they help each other take care of their young.

▲ **Crows in a large group call out to one another in order to stay together.**

Being part of a group means staying in touch with others. Crows do this through their calls. Each call is a combination of sounds with its own meaning. One call might mean "Feed me, Mommy!" Another might mean "Stay away!" Still another might mean "An **enemy** is near! Come and help!"

The main sound that a crow makes is "caw." Different combinations of caws have different meanings.

▲ **The pied crow looks different from the American crow because of its white chest. However, the sounds that it makes are very similar.**

# Mobbing an Enemy

*Caw! Caw! Caw!* A chorus of harsh cries fills the air. More and more crows gather in the sky. They circle around a tree. One after another, they swoop down on something hidden within its branches. The crows are taking part in an activity called **mobbing**.

The action begins when one crow spots an owl or another enemy. The bird sends out an **assembly call**, telling other crows to join in. Soon dozens of screaming crows are surrounding the enemy. They go on mobbing it until their noisy teamwork drives it away.

◀ The great horned owl is the crow's main enemy. These large owls hunt crows at night.

Mockingbirds and blackbirds sometimes mob crows.

◀ Crows usually mob owls, such as the one shown in the circle. They can also mob hawks, raccoons, and foxes.

19

# At the Nest

In spring, male and female crows pair up. Together, they build a cozy nest. When she is ready, the female lays three to seven eggs.

Like many birds, crows are good parents. They protect, feed, and teach their young. Crow families are different from most other bird families in one important way, however.

Many crow families include young birds that act as "babysitters." These helpers bring food to the hungry babies. They also help guard the nest. Scientists think that having helpers is a smart thing to do. Baby crows have a better chance of surviving when helpers pitch in.

Living with a crow family helps the babysitters, too. They get on-the-job training that will come in handy when they become parents themselves.

▲ **The young crows who act as helpers are usually older brothers or sisters of the new babies.**

◄ **Baby crows are always hungry. Like adult crows, they will eat almost anything.**

# Fun and Games

It's time to play King of the Castle! One crow stands on a rock and holds a stick in his mouth. Another tries to grab the stick and take it away. If he can, then he'll win the game.

▲ **Sticks are useful for building nests. They also come in handy when it's time to play.**

Crows also like to play catch and tug-of-war with twigs and sticks.

Young crows love to play. Their playfulness does not show that they are silly, though. In fact, it shows that they're smart. Scientists say that playing helps an animal learn important lessons. The crows playing King of the Castle are learning skills that will help them nab food from other animals.

▲ **This crow has just stolen an egg from another bird. Many crows learn this skill from playing games where they snatch twigs from other crows.**

# Looking and Learning

What else do crows do for fun? They sometimes do loop-the-loops and other **daredevil** stunts as they fly. Sometimes they swing upside down from a branch. One crow even invented a new version of surfing. The bird rode down a grassy hill while perched on a squashed plastic cup.

If one crow sees another trying out a fancy new game or trick, the bird will probably try it out, too. By doing so, the crow shows his ability to learn, which is a sure sign of intelligence. The crow even manages to learn while having fun. What could be smarter?

▲ **Crows enjoy doing stunts as they fly through the air.**

People in Alaska have seen crows sledding. The crows break chunks of snow off rooftops and use them to sled down the roofs.

◀ **Crows learn many things from one another, including where to find food, what dangers to avoid, and how to have fun.**

# Smart Stories

For centuries, people from many **cultures** have watched crows and told stories about their cleverness. In stories from Native American cultures, the crow and its relative, the raven, are powerful spirits. The actions of these birds are often bold and playful.

◄ The raven and the crow play important parts in the stories and artwork of many Native American peoples. This raven totem pole can be seen in one of Alaska's national parks.

Today scientists and other crow-watchers are learning that crows in fact do many clever things. They make tools. They solve problems and score high on tests. They play tricks on others but have shown that they are not easily fooled. The evidence is piling up. Crows really are smart animals with a special sense of **mischief** and fun.

Most scientists agree that the crow and the raven are probably the smartest of all birds. The only bird that may be as smart is the parrot.

# Just the Facts

|  | **American Crow** | **Common Raven** |
|---|---|---|
|  |  |  |
| **Length** (from head to tail) | 17–21 inches (43–53 cm) | 27 inches (69 cm) |
| **Weight** | 1 pound (454 g) | 1½ pounds (680 g) |
| **Wingspan** | 3 feet (.9 m) | 4 feet (1.2 m) |
| **Life Span** | 10 years | 15 years |
| **Habitat** | cities, suburbs, and rural areas in North America | rural areas, especially mountains, in North America, Asia, and Europe |
| **Food** | a wide variety, including seeds, fruit, nuts, insects, eggs, mice, small birds, and worms | a wide variety, including seeds, fruit, nuts, insects, eggs, mice, lizards, small birds, and snakes |

# More Smart Crows

Crows help other crows who are in need. Scientists have described one especially kind crow. He kept stopping by to bring food to an injured crow while collecting food for his family.

Aesop, a famous ancient Greek storyteller, told about a clever crow in one of his fables. The crow wanted to drink water from a pitcher. The bird could not reach the small amount that was left at the bottom, though. So the crow filled the pitcher with pebbles. Now the water reached the top, and the crow could drink it!

# Glossary

**assembly call**
(uh-SEM-blee KAWL)
a call that a crow makes to get other crows to gather together

**beak** (BEEK) the hard, horn-shaped part of a bird's mouth

**corvid** (KOR-vid) the family of birds that includes crows, ravens, jays, and magpies

**cultures** (KUHL-churz) the customs and traditions shared by a group of people

**daredevil** (DAIR-*dev*-il) dangerous or risky

**enemy** (EN-uh-mee) someone who wants to harm someone else

**experiment** (ek-SPER-uh-ment) a scientific test set up to find the answer to a question

**habitat** (HAB-uh-*tat*) a place in nature where an animal is normally found

**intelligence** (in-TEL-uh-juhns) the ability to understand, solve problems, and learn

**mimics** (MIM-iks) animals or people who can copy the sounds and actions of other things

**mischief** (MISS-chif) playful behavior that may cause trouble

**mobbing** (MOB-ing) crows noisily gathering around an enemy in order to chase it away

**predators** (PRED-uh-turz) animals that hunt other animals for food

**roadkill** (ROHD-kil) an animal that has been killed on the road by a car or other moving vehicle

**scarecrows** (SKAIR-krohz) stuffed dolls that look like people and are put in fields to scare crows away

**scavengers** (SKAV-uhn-juhrz) animals that feed on the dead bodies of other animals

**social** (SOH-shuhl) living in groups and having contact with others

**species** (SPEE-sheez) groups that animals are divided into, according to similar characteristics; members of the same species can have offspring

**tool** (TOOL) a piece of equipment that is used to do a job

# Bibliography

**Kilham, Lawrence.** *The American Crow and the Common Raven.* College Station, TX: Texas A&M University Press (1989).

**Savage, Candace.** *Bird Brains: The Intelligence of Crows, Ravens, Magpies, and Jays.* San Francisco, CA: Sierra Club Books (1997).

**Sax, Boria.** *Crow.* London: Reaktion Books (2004).

http://users.ox.ac.uk/~kgroup/tools/tools_main.shtml

# Read More

**Facklam, Margery.** *What Does the Crow Know? The Mysteries of Animal Intelligence.* San Francisco, CA: Sierra Club Books for Children (1994).

**Johnson, Sylvia A.** *Crows.* Minneapolis, MN: Carolrhoda Books (2004).

**Nichols, Catherine.** *Animal Masterminds.* Danbury, CT: Children's Press (2003).

**Pringle, Laurence.** *Crows! Strange and Wonderful.* Honesdale, PA: Boyds Mills Press (2002).

# Learn More Online

Visit these Web sites to learn more about crows:

http://wildwnc.org/af/americancrow.html

www.sciencenewsforkids.org/articles/20050119/Note3.asp

# Index

## About the Author

Natalie Lunis has written over two dozen science and nature books for children. She watches and learns from crows in the New York City area.